MONSTERS

KILLER SHARKS

BY LORI MORTENSEN

KIDHAVEN PRESS
A part of Gale, Cengage Learning

GALE
CENGAGE Learning™

Detroit • New York • San Francisco • New Haven, Conn • Waterville, Maine • London

GALE
CENGAGE Learning

© 2008 Gale, Cengage Learning

LIBRARY OF CONGRESS CATALOGING-IN-PUBLICATION DATA

Mortensen, Lori, 1955-
    Killer sharks / by Lori Mortensen.
        p. cm. — (Monsters)
    Includes bibliographical references and index.
    ISBN 978-0-7377-4044-8 (hardcover)
    1. Shark attacks. 2. Sharks. I. Title.
    QL638.93.M67 2008
    597.3—dc22
                                                                 2008006128

KidHaven Press
27500 Drake Rd
Farmington Hills MI 48331

ISBN-13: 978-0-7377-4044-8
ISBN-10: 0-7377-4044-2

Printed in the United States of America
1 2 3 4 5 6 7 12 11 10 09 08

CONTENTS

CHAPTER 1

VILLAINS OF THE SEA

It was a disturbing image. While a woman swam peacefully on the surface of the sea, a monster surged up from the inky depths beneath her. Its gaping jaws revealed murderous rows of sharp, jagged teeth. People who saw it knew the woman was doomed. In a split second, the deadly creature would devour her with one horrific bite of its razor-sharp teeth. *Crunch!*

This terrifying image was displayed on posters and advertisements for the 1975 horror movie *Jaws.* Audiences everywhere sat transfixed as their worst nightmare—being eaten alive—played out in living color on big screens around the world. It was particularly horrifying because the monster of this movie

The terrifying motion picture from the terrifying No. 1 best seller.

JAWS

ROY SCHEIDER   ROBERT SHAW   RICHARD DREYFUSS

JAWS

The 1975 movie Jaws made audiences think twice before entering the water for a swim.

was not a fictional creature like Godzilla or King Kong. The monster of this movie was a shark.

Sharks are real **predators** that have been roaming the seas for more than 400 million years. Their image is so menacing that experts believe the word *shark* may have come from the word *schurke,* the German word for "villain."

What Is a Shark?

In spite of this terrifying reputation as a monster, sharks are fish. They live in oceans all over the world. Most live in tropical waters, although some live in the frigid waters of the Arctic and Antarctica as well.

Like other fish, sharks have a backbone; breathe with gills; and have streamlined bodies, fins, and tails. Over thousands of years, however, many sharks have **evolved** in ways that have made them especially dangerous predators.

No Bones About It

One difference between sharks and other fish is their skeleton. While most fish have skeletons made of bone, a shark's skeleton is made of **cartilage**. Cartilage is firm, yet flexible. It is the same stuff that makes up a person's nose and ears.

While skeletons made of bones hold their shape, skeletons of cartilage bend. This makes it easier for sharks to attack. Many divers have discovered this after gently pulling on the tail of a

small, resting shark. Instead of scurrying away or ignoring the diver, the shark suddenly twists around and bites the intruder.

Toothy Skin

Shark skin can be dangerous, too. Unlike a fish's smooth scales, shark skin is covered with thousands of tiny teeth called **dermal denticles**. For most sharks, the dermal denticles lie flat, pointing toward the tail. When the skin is stroked from head to tail, the skin feels smooth. But if the skin is stroked in the opposite direction, the denticles poke up, making the skin feel rough. The skin of some sharks is so rough, it can scratch and tear a person's skin. Sharks may also use their skin to wound prey.

Swimming Noses

Sharks' sense of smell also helps them catch prey. Their sense of smell is so sensitive, sharks are sometimes called "swimming noses." Since they

Sharks have a powerful sense of smell and can detect scents up to a mile away.

breathe through their gills, sharks use their noses only for smelling.

To locate scents, sharks swing their heads back and forth in the water as they swim. By leading with one nostril, then the other, a shark can discover where a scent is coming from. Sharks can detect scents up to a mile away, and once located, follow it for miles.

Lateral Line

Like other fish, sharks also have another sensory system called the **lateral line**. The lateral line detects vibrations, so it acts much like a human ear. But the lateral line does not stick out in the water like ears would. Instead, the lateral line is a faint line of sensory nerves that runs along both sides of the shark from head to tail.

Sharks use the lateral lines to detect even the tiniest vibrations in the water—from waves lapping on the shore to the irregular vibrations of wounded prey. Pores on the shark's snout, part of the lateral line, lead to special organs that detect electricity. Because all living things give off tiny amounts of electricity, this is another powerful tool sharks can use to locate their prey.

The Perfect Eating Machine

Sharks have a lot of tools for catching prey, but it is their mouth that makes this animal one of the deadliest fish in the sea. Sharks are so deadly, in fact, they have been called the perfect eating machine.

This great white shark's sharp and jagged teeth are deadly.

A shark's mouth is different from other animals' mouths in two important ways. Like most animals, sharks have a lower jaw that is not attached directly to the skull. Because of this, the jaw can open and shut. Unlike other animals, however, a shark's upper jaw is unattached, too. This arrangement allows the shark to open its mouth very wide and thrust its jaws forward as it bites.

Sharks also do not have a single row of teeth like other animals do. Instead, they have rows of teeth that move as if they were on a **conveyor belt**. As teeth break or fall out, new ones advance forward to replace them. Some sharks may lose as many as

30,000 teeth a year. "The sharks have succeeded," wrote **paleontologist** Edwin H. Colbert in *Evolution of the Vertebrates,* "because . . . they have been very aggressive fishes, quite capable of taking care of themselves, in spite of earth changes, changes in food supply, and competitors."[1]

Because sharks are known as deadly predators, it would be easy to believe all sharks are dangerous to people. But they are not. Experts believe there are about 450 different species of sharks. No one

knows the exact number because three to five new shark species are discovered each year. Some species, such the **pygmy** shark, may be as small as a loaf of bread. Others, such as the whale shark, may be as long as a school bus. In fact, the whale shark is the biggest fish in the sea.

Though the whale shark is large and menacing in appearance, it uses its huge gaping mouth for eating the tiniest of sea creatures: plankton.

But an increase in size does not necessarily equal an increase in danger to people. Some large sharks, like the whale shark with its huge gaping mouth, feed on the tiniest creatures of the sea—**plankton**. And although the image of a shark's fin in the water instantly brings on feelings of fear, there are only about 100 shark attacks per year worldwide. Of these, fifteen are fatal. More people are killed by bee stings or lightning strikes than by shark attacks. Yet certain species of sharks are dangerous and have terrorized the sea since prehistoric times.

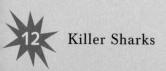

CHAPTER 2

ANCIENT PREDATORS

If people were asked to name the most deadly predator that ever lived, most would say *Tyrannosaurus rex* or *Velociraptor*, featured in movies such as *Jurassic Park*. *Tyrannosaurus rex* was a huge, lizardlike creature with sharp, gnashing teeth and a powerful tail. *Velociraptor*, although smaller than *Tyrannosaurus rex*, was a terrifying dinosaur with long, slashing claws. Yet there was another creature unmatched for destructive power in the prehistoric world.

CARCHARODON MEGALODON

This powerful creature was a shark called **Carcharodon megalodon** that some experts believe lived 16 to 1.6 million years ago. Its name means "rough tooth"

This giant prehistoric shark jaw, on display at an auction in 2004, contains 182 fossil teeth.

or "huge tooth." Although the longest shark tooth today is about 2 inches (5cm) long, fossil remains of *Carcharodon megalodon*'s triangular teeth are an astonishing 8 inches (20cm) long—about as big as a man's hand. Experts believe this prehistoric shark was longer than a city bus and weighed more than ten elephants.

Over time, *Carcharodon megalodon* became extinct like other prehistoric creatures. Yet its descendants continued to roam the seas, terrorizing people for thousands of years.

Gods of the Sea

Sharks were so deadly and powerful that long ago people of the Pacific Islands believed sharks were gods that lived in the depths of the sea. According to one Pacific Island legend, the sharks turned into shark men called **mano-kanoka**. Once in human form, the creatures traveled through the islands causing mischief. Some legends said that the sharks changed into men to lure unsuspecting islanders into the sea. Once there, the men turned back into sharks and the islanders were never seen again.

Human Sacrifices

Other Pacific Island legends say that shark gods required human sacrifice. The high priest and a helper would walk among the people. As they traveled, the helper carried a noose. After a sign from the priest, the helper would fling the noose over the crowd. Whoever the noose caught was strangled on the spot, cut into pieces, and thrown into the sea to feed the **voracious** shark gods.

In the Solomon Islands, people once built caverns for shark gods to live in. People built sacrificial altars made of stone in front of the caves. The bodies of the chosen victims were placed on the altar where special ceremonies were performed. At the end of the ceremony, the bodies were fed to the sharks.

Other legends tell of people worshipping a particular kind of shark. William Ellis, a missionary who preached in the Society Islands during the early nineteenth century, reported this practice. "Rather than destroy the great blue sharks," he wrote, "they would endeavor to [gain] their favor by prayers and offerings. Temples were erected in which priests [led ceremonies], and offerings were presented to the **deified** sharks, while fishermen and others, who were much at sea, sought their favor."[2]

ANCESTORS AND WIZARDS

Sharks were not always seen as demanding, vengeful gods, however. According to other legends in the Solomon Islands, sharks were good. People believed sharks were dead ancestors that had returned in the form of a shark. Instead of hurting people, the **reincarnated** sharks protected their relatives.

According to legends of the Tanga Islands, sharks were dangerous wizards. The wizards were so dangerous, people were not allowed to hunt them. This belief probably got started when people

used snares to hunt sharks from their canoes. But instead of capturing the sharks, the sharks often dragged the hunters and their canoes away—and the hunters were never seen again. Although it is not possible to know which sharks inspired the beliefs about shark gods and wizards, many of these beliefs and legends were probably based on the human-eating sharks we know today.

GREAT WHITE SHARKS

Experts believe many legends were based on great white sharks. These sharks are the largest predatory fish in the sea. Some experts believe great white sharks are descendants of *Carcharodon megalodon.*

Great white sharks are called different names in different parts of the world. Sometimes they are called "white pointers," "white shark," or "white death." Great white sharks can grow up to 20 feet (6m) long and weigh about 3,000 pounds (1,361kg). Unconfirmed reports say they may grow up to 30 feet (9m) long and weigh 7,000 pounds (3,175kg).

Great white sharks are gray on top and white underneath. This coloration protects them better than if they were all white, as their name implies. The white on the belly helps them to blend in with the light colors when seen from below. The gray on top helps them to blend in with the dark color of the sea when seen from above. Fighter planes use this same coloring so they will be less visible in the sky.

To catch its prey, the great white shark lunges out of the water with terrific force.

Killer Sharks

A great white shark's diet includes seals, sea lions, and dolphins. To catch its meal, the great white shark sneaks up beneath its prey as the unsuspecting creature swims near the surface. Suddenly, the shark rockets out of the water and grabs hold of its prey in its sharp, jagged teeth. After that first bite, the shark releases its victim and circles around. When the prey is weak, the shark returns and devours its meal.

TIGER SHARKS

Although great white sharks have a reputation for being the deadliest shark, many others are known human-eaters. One of the fiercest is the tiger shark, so named because of its silvery vertical stripes and

Tiger sharks are among the fiercest predators in the ocean.

aggressive behavior. Armed with serrated, sickle-shaped teeth, the tiger shark's diet includes other sharks, rays, sea birds, dolphins, turtles, and dead whales. Yet these sharks also have a habit of eating almost anything, making them a particularly dangerous predator.

Often called the "swimming garbage can," tiger sharks have devoured such things as coal, suits of armor, kegs of nails, rolls of tar paper, raincoats, and license plates. To get rid of indigestible items, tiger sharks turn their stomachs inside out, spewing the contents back into the sea.

Bull Sharks

Bull sharks are also known as human-eaters. Since they can live in fresh or salt water, they are found in oceans, lakes, and rivers. Bull sharks have been seen as far as 2,300 miles (3,702m) up the Amazon River. They grow to about 11 feet (3m) long and weigh about 670 pounds (304kg). Many scientists believe bull sharks are the most dangerous sharks to humans. This is because they swim in the shallow waters in rivers and along the coasts, where people are plentiful.

Oceanic Whitetips

Still, the shark known to attack more people than all other sharks is called the oceanic whitetip. These sharks get their name from their broad fins tipped with white. Known for their fearlessness and ag-

Bull sharks swim in shallow waters along coastlines, which makes them a danger to people.

gression, they grow to about 13 feet (4m) long and weigh about 370 pounds (168kg).

One of the most gruesome attacks by oceanic whitetips occurred in 1945 when the USS *Indianapolis* sailed to the Philippines during World War II. On July 28 a Japanese submarine torpedoed the cruiser, sinking the ship. Of nearly 1,200 men, 850 survived the blast and floated in the water on life rafts waiting to be rescued.

At dawn, oceanic whitetips began their attack. Survivors recorded between 25 and 88 shark attacks. Day after day, the sharks kept coming. When rescuers finally arrived four days later, only 318 men were left. More than 500 had perished, most of them by shark attacks.

 Killer Sharks

CHAPTER 3

SHARK ATTACK!

No one knows how many people have been attacked by sharks. People have had deadly encounters with sharks for thousands of years. One of the earliest records of a shark attack appeared in a 1580 issue of the *Fugger News-Letter,* a forerunner of the modern newspaper. An article contained a seaman's gripping eyewitness account of what happened while he was sailing between India and Portugal.

When a man fell from our ship into the sea during a strong wind, so that we could not wait for him or come to his rescue in any other fashion, we threw out to him on a rope a wooden block, especially prepared for that purpose, and this he finally managed to grasp and thought he could save himself thereby. But when our crew drew this block with the man toward the ship and had him within half the carrying distance of a musket shot, there appeared from below the surface of the sea a large monster called **Tiburon**; it rushed on the man and tore him to pieces before our very eyes. That surely was a grievous death.[3]

Horrible tales of shark attacks, some exaggerated and some true, were very common among sailors in the 1600s and 1700s.

Many ships' logs included encounters with sharks. Because ships dumped galley garbage into the sea as they sailed, hungry sharks would follow behind the ships, sometimes for weeks. "They are the dread of all sailors in all hot climates," wrote naturalist Thomas Pennant in 1776, "where they constantly attend the ships in expectation of what might drop overboard; a man that has this misfortune inevitably perishes; they have been seen to dart at him, like a **gudgeon** to a worm."[4]

By the late 1800s sailors' tragic tales about human-eating sharks were dismissed as superstition and myth. Times were changing. Victorian society began looking to science for answers. Monsters of the deep were no more real than the great sea creatures depicted in Jules Verne's popular fiction adventure book, *Twenty Thousand Leagues Under the Sea.*

ATTACKS OF 1916

This belief was shattered in the summer of 1916 when sharks appeared along the Atlantic coast. The first attack occurred on July 1 when a young man named Charles Vansant swam with his dog out beyond the breakers near the Engleside Hotel in New Jersey. The first hint of trouble was when his dog swam back to shore. Vansant called his dog, but when it would not come back, he began swimming back to shore, too.

Soon, someone in the gathering crowd noticed a dark fin in the water. "Watch out!" the bystander

cried. In only 3.5 feet (1.1m) of water, it looked as if Vansant would make it. But before he reached the shore, great jaws exploded out of the water and bit him below the knee. His screams echoed over the beach while the crowd watched in horror.

"Most Horrible Death I Ever Saw"

As Vansant struggled to free himself, a young man came to his rescue. After the shark released its jaws, the young man began pulling Vansant ashore. But before he got there, the shark attacked again, clamping onto Vansant's thigh. Rescuers began a tug-of-war between Vansant and the shark. By the time rescuers pulled him to shore, his left leg was nearly torn off.

Witnesses argued about what could have caused such a horrible attack. Some thought a giant tuna ravaged his leg. Others said it was a giant sea turtle, capable of snapping a man in half.

When Vansant died of his wounds an hour later, a doctor concluded he died of a shark bite. It was the first time in U.S. history that a shark bite was listed as the official cause of death. One witness reported, "Mr. Vansant's death was the most horrible I ever saw."[5]

Two days later the *New York Times* published the incident on the last page with the headline, "Dies After Attack by Fish."[6] But people were not ready to believe it. They thought the newspaper had made it up and the man probably drowned. People

Killer Sharks

Even though shark attacks against people are fairly rare, just the idea of a shark attack can cause great panic and fear among the public.

associated swimming in the ocean with leisure and entertainment.

LAST SWIM

Despite the tragedy, five days later a popular swimmer named Charles Bruder swam straight out to sea. He was eager to show his friends he was not afraid of sharks.

In areas where shark attacks are known to occur, it is best to exercise caution before entering the water.

Killer Sharks

Minutes later, an unseen force yanked him beneath the waves. Bruder told the people who pulled him from the water:

He was a big, gray fellow and as rough as sandpaper. I didn't see him until after he struck me the first time. He cut me here in the side, and his belly was so rough it bruised my face and arms. That was when I yelled the first time. I thought he had gone on, but he only turned and shot back at me [and] . . . snipped my left leg off. . . . He yanked me clear under before he let go. . . . He came back at me again . . . and shook me like a terrier shakes a rat. But he let go while I was calling, then suddenly . . . he took off the other leg. He's a big fellow and awful hungry.[7]

Ten minutes later, Bruder died of his wounds, both legs gone.

For the first time, officials sounded an alarm up and down the beach. Thousands of people rushed to get out of the water.

Hunt for a Bloodthirsty Monster

Between July 1 and July 12, 1916, five swimmers were attacked along 80 miles of waterways of the New Jersey Atlantic Ocean coastline. Four died; one survived. The attacks fueled the ideas about sharks as bloodthirsty monsters tantalized by the taste of human flesh.

To stop the killer shark, fishermen set up metal nets and hunted the waters with boat hooks, harpoons, rifles, and dynamite. Finally, on July 14, a taxidermist named Michael Schleisser caught a 7.5 foot (2m) shark near Raritan Bay, clubbing it to death with a broken oar. Its stomach contained human remains. The fish was a great white shark.

Jaws

The image of a shark as a monster was reignited in 1975 when the horror movie *Jaws* was released in theaters around the country. The movie was based on Peter Benchley's book, *Jaws,* inspired by the attacks of 1916. Audiences around the world watched with a mixture of horror and fascination as a 25-foot-long (7.62m) great white shark annihilated innocent victims.

Model Monster

Filmmakers created this monster by mixing shots of real sharks filmed in Australia with images of three mechanical sharks. One was a full model attached to special rigging for underwater shots. Two were models of half sharks. One turned from left to right with machinery exposed on the left. The other turned right to left with machinery exposed on the right.

The killer shark earned *Jaws* two Academy Awards and won the number 18 spot on the American Film Institute's *100 Years, 100 Heroes and Villains* list.

The mechanical great white shark model built for the movie Jaws *(pictured), struck fear in the hearts of moviegoers everywhere.*

Jaws generated such a terrible image of sharks, however, it became "the most feared and loathed animal in modern history."[8] Fishermen in the United States, Australia, and South Africa began slaughtering sharks like never before.

CHAPTER 4

MISUNDERSTOOD MONSTER

Today scientists know much more about sharks than they did at the turn of the century or during the filming of *Jaws*. Sharks are no more villainous than any other predator on land or at sea. Any species that survives must be able to hunt and defend itself. Like other animals, sharks hunt to eat and attack when threatened.

But swimmers in open water are often unaware when they have crossed a shark's path. They do not see a warning color, observe a warning behavior, hear a warning sound, or smell a warning scent. When a shark attacks, it seems as if it comes out of nowhere, which adds to its reputation as a frightening monster. "The water does not belong to

32

human beings," said naturalist George Burgess. "When you're entering the ocean, you're entering the wilderness. It's not jumping in your pool in the backyard."[9]

MISTAKEN IDENTITY

In spite of the image that *Jaws* created of killer sharks feasting on people, sharks are not interested in people as food. Experts now believe shark attacks are a result of mistaken identity. When people swim on the surface of the water or surfers lie on their surfboards, predatory sharks mistake them for sea lions or turtles. Since sharks have evolved on an oceanic diet, they have not developed a taste for people.

Some experts believe a shark attack may occur when the shark mistakes a human for a sea creature, like this albatross.

When predatory sharks discover unfamiliar prey, they circle and then bump into it. This approach helps sharks evaluate whether it is something they would like to eat or not. If a shark believes it is a potential meal, it will take a bite. Some sharks are so big, however, one bite can be fatal to humans.

Shark Repellents

The U.S. government began developing shark repellents during World War II. It was important because servicemen sailed in shark-infested waters. The shark repellent would repel sharks much as insect repellents discouraged mosquitoes from biting.

Government scientists experimented with 78 different substances. Finally they selected a chemical that smelled like dead sharks. After tests showed it worked, the government called the repellent Shark Chasers and attached packets of it to life jackets. If a serviceman found himself in shark-infested waters, he would open the packet and swish it around in the water. The chemicals in the packet would stain the sea with blue-black clouds.

The government later discovered that the packets were not as effective as they had hoped. Sharks in water bloodied by whale kills ate the packets along with the whales during their feeding frenzies. Even though it did not work very well, having any kind of shark repellent made sailors feel safer than having nothing at all.

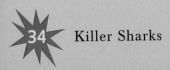

Moses Sole

Scientists also studied a flat fish that lives in the Red Sea. The flat fish is called **Moses sole**. As soon as a shark bites a Moses sole, it immediately swims away. Scientists discovered that when the Moses sole was attacked, it secreted a milky white toxin. Scientists tried to use this liquid to protect humans from sharks. But they discovered it did not work because the substance washed away too easily.

Studies with the Moses sole, however, led scientists to experiment with another substance—soap—that affected the water in the same way as the toxin produced by the Moses sole. Scientists discovered that squirts of concentrated soap irritated some sharks' gills enough to make them swim away.

SharkPODs

Another promising repellent is the SharkPOD (Protective Oceanic Device) that emits an electronic field. Since sharks are sensitive to electricity, this device works by forming something like an electronic cloud around the wearer. Currently the device is the size of a football and is strapped to scuba tanks. Researchers hope to make it as small as a calculator so that divers can wear it around their waists.

The most effective methods for preventing shark attacks are physical barriers, such as fences

An electronic shark repellent like this one may be useful for protecting divers against shark attacks.

and metal cages with bars, that protect divers while they are in the ocean. Unfortunately, fencing entire coastlines is not possible, so scientists are still looking for effective ways to repel sharks and prevent attacks.

Do We Need Sharks?

Some sharks are so dangerous that people might think the ocean would be better without them. But sharks are an important part of the oceanic food chain. Sharks in the ocean, like wolves, bears, and cougars in the wilderness, keep populations in check and remove old and diseased individuals. The consequences of losing a predator have been especially clear where people have removed deer's natural predators in the wilderness. Without predators to

Sharks are an important part of the oceanic food chain, yet are in danger of being overfished by humans.

keep their numbers in check, the deer population exploded. Deer overgrazed the food supply, forcing many to die from starvation and disease.

While no one knows exactly what would happen if great white sharks were removed from the top of the food chain, experts believe it would have devastating consequences. They do know what happened when a shark fishery in Tasmania overfished sharks. When the sharks were gone, the spiny lobsters disappeared, too. People did not know that the survival of the spiny lobsters was linked to the survival of the sharks. After the sharks were gone, there was no predator to keep the octopus population in check. Octopus multiplied and wiped out their prey—lobsters.

As scientists continue to explore the world of sharks and find ways to prevent attacks, people are also creating global organizations to protect sharks from senseless slaughter. While ten to fifteen people are killed each year by sharks, over 100 million sharks perish at the hands of humans each year. Experts believe the population of sharks has decreased by 90 percent worldwide over the past 50 years. Sharks are killed to make fin soup, cosmetics, medicines, liver oil, and ornaments made from their teeth and jaws.

SHARK TALES

Even though most people will never encounter a shark in the ocean, sharks have a firm grip on modern culture. Most recently sharks have appeared in

Killer Sharks

From atop a billboard, "Bruce," the shark from the hit 2003 movie Finding Nemo, *grins from gill to gill.*

popular movies such as Disney's 2003 *Finding Nemo* followed by DreamWorks's 2004 hit *Shark Tales*. In each movie, artists used details of real sharks to create memorable characters in fun action adventures across the big screen.

Other modern-day sightings in culture include riveting books about sharks, such as *Shark Life: True Stories about Sharks and the Sea* by *Jaws* author Benchley, and exciting shark figures, models, shark reef aquariums, and images on T-shirts, sleepwear, and swim trunks.

Yet no matter how familiar sharks may become in popular culture, there will always be an aura of mystery surrounding them. "People are, and always have been," wrote Benchley, "simultaneously intrigued and terrified by sharks. Sharks come from a wing of the dark castle where our nightmares live—deep water beyond our sight and understanding—and so they stimulate our fears and fantasies and imaginations."[10]

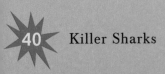

Killer Sharks

NOTES

CHAPTER 1: VILLAINS OF THE SEA

1. Quoted in Thomas Allen, *The Shark Almanac.* New York: Lyons, 1999, p. 10.

CHAPTER 2: ANCIENT PREDATORS

2. Quoted in Allen, *The Shark Almanac,* p. 208.

CHAPTER 3: SHARK ATTACK!

3. Quoted in Allen, *The Shark Almanac,* p. 215.
4. Quoted in "Shark History," www.shark-info.com.
5. Quoted in Michael Capuzzo, *The Terrifying Shark Attacks of 1916.* New York: Crown, 2003, p. 37.
6. Quoted in Capuzzo, p. 40.
7. Quoted in Capuzzo, p. 55.
8. Quoted in Allen, *The Shark Almanac,* p. 82.

CHAPTER 4: MISUNDERSTOOD MONSTER

9. Quoted in Allen, *The Shark Almanac,* p. 173.
10. Quoted in Peter Benchley, *Shark Trouble.* New York: Random House, 2002, p. xi.

GLOSSARY

Carcharodon megalodon: A giant prehistoric shark that lived between 16 to 1.6 million years ago, believed to be the biggest meat-eating fish that ever lived.

cartilage: A strong, flexible type of connective tissue.

conveyor belt: A mechanical device with a continuously moving belt that moves materials from one place to another.

deified: Made into a god.

dermal denticles: Small outgrowths on the skin of many fish similar to teeth.

evolve: To slowly change or grow over time.

gudgeon *(GUJ-en)***:** A small freshwater fish.

lateral line: A sensory system of pores located at the head and along the sides of fish that detects minute vibrations in the water.

mano-kanoka: Legendary creatures with human mothers and shark gods as fathers.

Moses sole: A small, flat fish that lives in the Red Sea. It produces a toxin that repels sharks.

paleontologist: Someone who studies prehistoric life through plant and animal fossils.

plankton: From the Greek word *planktos,* meaning "wanderer." Refers to any tiny organism that drifts in bodies of water.

predators: Living things that eat other living things.

pygmy: Refers to a group of short people in Central Africa who generally grow no taller than 4 feet, 11 inches (1.5m). The word is also sometimes used to describe the smaller types of a species of animal.

reincarnated: The state of being reborn in another body after dying.

Tiburon: The Spanish word for shark.

voracious: Having a huge appetite.

FOR FURTHER EXPLORATION

BOOKS

Berger, Melvin and Gilda, *Scholastic Question and Answer: What Do Sharks Eat for Dinner?* New York: Scholastic, 2001. A question-and-answer format allows readers to dive into the fascinating world of these extraordinary predators of the sea.

Wagner, Kathi, *Everything Kids' Shark Book: Dive Into Fun-Infested Waters.* Cincinnati: Adams Media, 2005. Readers learn amazing shark facts as they explore the world of sharks through exciting puzzles, mazes, and other do-it-yourself activities.

Wexo, John Bonnett, *Sharks.* Peru, Il: Zoobooks, 2003. This book is packed with scientific facts, striking photographs, and illustrations that teach children everything they would want to know about this mysterious creature of the sea.

WEB SITES

Discovery Channel (www.dsc.discovery.com/sharks). This site features all sorts of information about sharks, especially during Shark Week, including the ultimate shark quiz, virtual dives with sharks, and a shark runner game.

Kidzone (www.kidzone.ws/sharks/index.htm). An array of fun shark facts, photos, and activities for readers through grade four can all be found on this Web site.

Monterey Bay Aquarium (www.mbayaq.org/). This site's features explore the myths and mysteries of sharks around the world and throughout history.

INDEX

P

Pacific islands
  sharks in legends of,
    15–17
Pennant, Thomas, 25
Plankton, 12
Pygmy shark, 11

S

Schleisser, Michael, 30
Shark attacks
  of 1916, 25–26, 28–30
  annual deaths from, 38
  earliest reports of,
    23–24
  first in U.S., 26
  as result of mistaken
    identity, 33–34
  in World War II,
    21–22
*Shark Life: True Stories
  about Sharks and the Sea*
  (Benchley), 39
Shark repellents, 34
Shark Tales (film), 39
SharkPOD (Protective
  Ocean Device), 35
Sharks
  characteristics of, 6

model of, for *Jaws,* 30
number of species of,
  10–11
in Pacific island
  legends, 15–17
as perfect eating
  machine, 8–10
prehistoric, 13, 15
role in oceanic food
  chain, 36, 38
sense of smell of, 7–8

T

Tiger sharks, 19–20
*Twenty Thousand Leagues
  Under the Sea* (Verne),
  25

U

USS *Indianapolis*
  (cruiser), 21–22

V

Vansant, Charles,
  25–26
Verne, Jules, 25

W

Whale shark, 11, 12

Picture Credits

About the Author

Lori Mortensen is a multi-published author of more than 100 stories and articles for children that have appeared in magazines such as *Highlights for Children, Ladybug, The Friend, Wild Outdoor World,* and many others. She has also written seven nonfiction books, including *The Sphinx* and *Leprechauns* in KidHaven Press's Monsters and Mysterious Encounters series. Mortensen lives in California with her family. Learn more about her and her books at www.lorimortensen.com.